HIRE ME!

Secrets of
Job
Interviewing

by

Patricia Noel Drain

D0967836

PRICE STERN SLOAN
Los Angeles

TABLE OF CONTENTS

PREFACE

Several years ago, a woman moved to a new city. She was looking for a wonderful opportunity with a growing company and enthusiastically started interviewing. She hadn't worked in 15 years, but believed everyone would see what an asset she would be for their company because she knew she was the type who would give 100 percent to any job.

Unfortunately, she discovered very quickly that there was more to interviewing than visiting with a potential employer, telling about her background, sharing what she wanted in a job, and living happily ever after. She also discovered that there was a lot of competition out there, and it wasn't always the best man or woman who wins.

Interviewers would ask, "Tell me about yourself," and she would speak at length about her husband, children, her former home, how long she'd been seeking a job, and other details of her life. Then they'd ask,

"Where do you see yourself in a year?" and she would reply, "I am really eager to succeed and hope to have a job like yours someday." Then when the issue of salary arose, she'd answer, "I'd like an annual salary of $36,000. Actually, I'd like $40,000, but I know you have to start somewhere." (This was a woman of ambition, especially since she'd never before made more than $15,000 a year.)

After each interview she'd once again find herself on the outside looking in. She'd wonder why she didn't get the job and where she'd gone wrong....

Well, that person was me. I knew, however, that there must be a better way, possibly some technique that would give me the edge over the others interviewing for the same position with no more desire or experience than I had.

Ironically, my first position was in the personnel industry, interviewing 10 to 20 candidates a week. Since that time, I have become a Certified Personnel Consultant and, through my company and public speaking opportunities, have been able to help hundreds of people avoid the silly mistakes I myself made so many years ago.

I also discovered over and over again that people need guidance through this difficult and sometime vulnerable stage in their lives called *interviewing*. Most people aren't in this predicament very often, but when they are, they need to know that they can't take it personally because *it's a numbers game*, and *it's a learned technique*. I share this information daily through our firm, seminars and speeches, but I feel the information is so vital that I decided to reach a broader audience through this book.

The following pages are filled with helpful hints that *I know work*. I know because the thousands of candidates I've sent on interviews have been offered their dream jobs when they put to use the concepts you are about to read.

So get ready for facts and techniques that can lead to the job *you* desire.

Successfully,

Patricia Noel Drain, CPC

THE 10 SECRETS OF SUCCESSFUL INTERVIEWING

Why do I call them secrets? Doesn't everyone know you set a time for an interview, meet with the prospective employer, are honest about your needs and expectations, then start working for that perfect company, and hope you match the employer's desires?

Wrong.

Oddly enough, both the candidate and the employer are basically looking for the same qualities in each other—they just don't know how to verbalize them. Those qualities are:

- Appreciation
- Dependability

- Stability
- Long-term commitment
- Team orientation
- Professionalism
- Loyalty

Amazing, isn't it? I bet these attributes describe you and the qualities you desire in your ideal company. Employers I've worked with describe what they look for in potential employees the same way. And the No. 1 item *everyone* is looking for, bar none, is to feel appreciated.

Now that you know that you and your potential employer are looking for the same thing, how do you find each other?

I don't believe in saving the best for last, so I have listed the 10 Secrets of Successful Interviewing on the next page.

When you've read them, you'll know the secrets that it took me years to discover. As we discuss each secret in detail, you will see more clearly what you can do to land your ideal job.

THE 10 SECRETS OF SUCCESSFUL INTERVIEWING

1. Make your resume short, simple and "*sizzling.*"

2. What you wear is as important as what you say.

3. Your body language sends "signals" to everyone you meet.

4. *First* and *last* impressions *do* count.

5. Always fill out company applications completely.

6. Interviewing is a numbers game, so know your numbers.

7. There are only 20 basic questions asked during any interview.

8. How you answer those 20 basic questions can give—or take away—your competitive edge.

9. Your purpose with *every* interview is to get an offer.

10. Second interviews are as important as the first.

SECRET #1

> **Make your resume short, simple and "*sizzling*."**

A resume is a company's first impression of a candidate. Your resume should reflect your personality and skills as closely as possible. Its purpose is to get your foot in the door for a person-to-person interview with the hiring authority.

Your resume should be short, succinct and, most importantly, have "*sizzle*." What is sizzle? Imagine that you are in a restaurant. The waiter appears with a sizzling steak platter and tells you to prepare for a feast. Your mouth begins watering, and you can't wait to savor the flavor. *That's sizzle.* Now that doesn't mean your written presentation of yourself should be corny or cute, but you should strive to make the employer anxious to meet you.

When applied to your experience, the list of action words found at the end of this chapter can give your resume sizzle.

Here are some other good tips about resumes:

- If you include an objective at the beginning of your resume, keep it generic enough so that you don't exclude yourself as a candidate for other positions within the company that might interest you.

- Organize your resume carefully. If it's logical and easy to absorb, your audience is more likely to read it.

- Unless you are trying to obtain a position in creative advertising or public relations, stick with white, light beige, bone or gray paper. Don't get too flashy, or you may draw unnecessary—and undesirable—attention to yourself.

- Resumes should be *one* page long. Descriptive words will help you keep your resume brief.

- Don't explain why you left each company. If the interviewer asks, be prepared to answer, but there's no need to mention it in the resume.

- Don't give dates—such as graduation dates—that give away your age. You only want to include information that will *encourage* a personal interview.

- Don't put salary requirements on your resume. If you are screening companies this way or a company asks for that information, include it in your cover letter.

- You should have at least two resumes emphasizing different areas of expertise. For instance, if you have managerial experience and computer capabilities, you should slant one resume toward your management skills and another toward your technical abilities.

Remember, the overriding rule in resume writing is to keep it simple enough to secure an interview. Once you get there, you can sell yourself. (If you don't think so, keep reading!)

Example A is a typical "easy to read" resume that states everything an employer needs to know about you and your background. Do not go back more than 10 years

---

JANE DOE
1234 S. 5th Street   *   Phoenix, Arizona 87654   *   (602) 123-4567

STATEMENT OF QUALIFICATIONS

Self-starter, action-oriented individual capable of independent decision-making and sound judgment. Able to work equally well with a wide variety of personalities. Eager to learn and tenacious in all endeavors.

EXPERIENCE

JCB Company   Phoenix, Arizona
Assistant Marketing Administrator   04/89 - Present
Aided in the production of in-house desktop publishing project to produce sales and marketing literature and correspondence for a network of national and international sales representatives.

Talent Search   Scottsdale, Arizona
Assistant Director   02/87 - 04/89
Responsible for the design, implementation and maintenance of the first companywide collection department. Computed and submitted all monthly reports and scheduled all bookings for the School of Talent and Modeling.

Professional Search   Tucson, Arizona
Administrative Assistant   04/85 - 02/87
Responsibilities included complete administrative support to company president. Aided Operations Manager with job files and bookkeeping. Established and maintained job project filing system.

TECHNICAL SKILLS

Typing 70 wpm, Microsoft Word 4.0 and 5.0, Leading Edge word processing. Paradox 3.0 and 3.5 database management software, elementary LOTUS 1-2-3.

EDUCATION

Arizona State University, Tempe, Arizona, BS
University of London, Study abroad student

REFERENCES

Available upon request.

Example A

THOMAS DOE
1234 S. 5th Street
Phoenix, AZ 87654
(602) 123-4567

OBJECTIVE

To secure a position with a progressive, innovative company where my skills and experience can be utilized to their fullest.

STRENGTHS

- Well-developed communication skills, including preparing job descriptions, fact sheets, speeches and resumes.

- Strong verbal communication skills, including extensive experience as an interviewer.

- Proficiency with computers and word processing.

- Professional development includes seminars in time management, sales, recruitment/interviewing and personal development.

EXPERIENCE

3/88-present MCI COMMUNICATIONS, Phoenix, AZ
Commercial Sales Representative
Responsible for contacting and providing information to prospective MCI customers. Preparation and presentation of sales proposals. Maintenance of accounts.

2/84-3/88 INDEPENDENT PERSONNEL, INC., Lincoln, NE
Personnel Consultant
Responsible for interviewing, screening, testing and preparing candidates for permanent job placement. Marketing personnel services to other companies. Servicing established accounts.

EDUCATION

University of Nebraska, Lincoln, NE
Bachelor of Science
Major: Marketing; Emphasis: Marketing Management

Example B

unless it pertains to a particular position.

Example B states the pertinent information clearly and succinctly. There are many ways to format your resume, but these two versions have worked well for our candidates over the years. Despite their differences, they are both *short, to the point, easy to follow* and *sizzling.*

FIRST THINGS FIRST

Do introduce your resume with a cover letter. The cover letter is the place to explain why you're sending your resume to them and, if necessary, to discuss salary requirements.

You can write several different cover letters or simply have one that is general enough to meet any company's qualifications. If you have access to a word processor or typewriter, personalize your cover letter by inserting a specific job title and a sentence or two about the position you are applying for or the company you are applying to.

JANE DOE
1234 S. 5th Street
Phoenix, AZ 87654
(602) 123-4567

December 12, 1992

Ms. Brenda Watkins
CAPITAL IDEA CORP.
44454 Pandare Pl.
Salt Lake City UT 55583

Dear Ms. Watkins:

I am interested in applying for the (type of position) opening at your company.

As my resume indicates, I have 15 years of experience. Among my greatest strengths are my organizational and supervisory skills as well as my attention to detail. On the technical side, I type 70 words per minute and have had extensive experience with a variety of computers and word processors.

I look forward to meeting with you at your earliest convenience to discuss the position. I will call you next week to schedule an appointment.

Thank you for your consideration

Sincerely,

Jane Doe
Jane Doe

An effective cover letter

SIZZLING WORDS FOR RESUMES

Accepted	Consulted	Implemented	Programmed
Accomplished	Contracted	Improved	Promoted
Achieved	Controlled	Increased	Proposed
Acquired	Coordinated	Initiated	Provided
Acted	Counseled	Inspected	Recommended
Adapted	Created	Installed	Reconciled
Administered	Demonstrated	Instructed	Recorded
Advised	Designed	Interpreted	Recruited
Allocated	Developed	Interviewed	Reduced (costs)
Analyzed	Diagnosed	Invented	Referred
Approved	Directed	Issued	Reorganized
Arranged	Displayed	Judged	Repaired
Assembled	Distributed	Launched	Reported
Assessed	Drafted	Located	Researched
Assisted	Drew	Maintained	Resolved
Attended	Edited	Managed	Restored
Audited	Enlarged	Manufactured	Reviewed
Balanced	Equipped	Medicated	Revised
Budgeted	Established	Monitored	Sanctioned
Charted	Estimated	Motivated	Scheduled
Classified	Evaluated	Negotiated	Secured
Cleaned	Exhibited	Observed	Sketched
Coached	Expanded	Obtained	Sold
Collected	Expedited	Operated	Studied
Communicated	Extended	Organized	Supervised
Compared	Facilitated	Painted	Supported
Compiled	Followed	Participated	Taught
Completed	Formulated	Performed	Trained
Composed	Founded	Planned	Translated
Computed	Fulfilled	Prepared	Updated
Concluded	Gathered	Presented	Won
Conducted	Generated	Printed	Wrote
Confirmed	Guided	Processed	
Constructed	Helped	Procured	
Contacted	Illustrated	Produced	

SECRET #2

```
What you wear is as
important as what
you say.
```

I'm going to get very specific in this chapter because I've learned to never assume anything.

Take, for instance, the lady who was going out on an interview for an administrative assistant position in a large corporation. I told her, "Wear something professional or, better yet, something you get a lot of compliments on." The day of the interview she walked into my office, resume in hand, in a *cocktail dress*...with feathers flowing from the back. I now get *specific* with everyone.

The following tips may seem elementary,

but being specific is better than being sorry!
Consider:

- The days of "Don't wear red,"
  "Black is power" are finally over.
  The one thing that hasn't changed
  is that wearing faddy, wild, large
  print and non-conservative outfits
  never works.

- Don't wear clothes that are too
  tight, too revealing, out of style or
  trendy.

- Details matter! It's the little things
  about your outfit (pins, tie tacks,
  pearls, scarves, etc.) that reflect
  your professional image.

- Avoid anything soiled or that
  wrinkles easily.

- Don't wear skirts or slacks that are
  too short. Skirts should be down to
  the knee, and slacks should touch
  the top of the shoes.

- Tennis shoes, sandals or shoes with
  straps are inappropriate. Make sure
  your shoes are shined and polished.

- Don't wear socks or nylons with
  holes or runs.

- Keep nails *short*, clean and
  manicured.

- Two squirts of perfume or

aftershave is enough.

- Avoid too much jewelry.
- Your hair should be clean and conservatively cut.

BRINGING IT ALL TOGETHER

Women look best in a suit and conservative blouse (nothing low cut, nothing see through). Patternless hose, (nude is best) and polished, unscuffed closed-toe pumps are preferred. Wear a moderate amount of makeup.

Men should wear a suit, long sleeved pressed shirt, a clean tie that hangs to the belt and shined shoes.

Suits are ideal for both men and women, because you can always take off the jacket if you are overdressed at a particular company. It is better to overdress rather than to dress inappropriately. The best bet is to investigate proper attire at the company before the interview by dropping by or asking someone who works there, but that isn't always possible.

Should you wear the same outfit to every interview? Yes, if it is a conservative, well-planned outfit. You will be seeing different people each initial meeting, so why not?

Most people think you have to be wealthy to look professional. What you really need is style. When shopping for the perfect interview outfit, just remember that you don't create a successful wardrobe by buying clothes you *like*, you do it by investing in clothing you *love*.

SECRET #3

> **Your body language sends signals to everyone you meet.**

For all the power of your words, you should know that your body language says things you might not be aware of—or mean—at all. These signals send messages to interviewers, who often actually look for such signs.

EYE CONTACT

It could be something as simple as shyness, but if you don't look directly at people, they think you are shifty and distrusting. Practice looking people right in the eye. It is very important in life in general, but especially during an interview.

HANDS BEHIND THE HEAD

You're probably just stretching or relaxing, but it looks like you don't care, or that you feel superior.

FINGERS UNDER THE CHIN

This is probably just a listening habit, but you appear skeptical and superior. Remember how the principal looked at you when you were called into the office?

ARMS FOLDED IN FRONT OF THE BODY

You could be cold or simply accustomed to sitting like that, but you appear unreceptive and closed-minded.

FIDDLING WITH TIE, SCARF OR PEN

This action makes you look unsure of

yourself. You could just be checking to make sure something is straight, but it suggests you are nervous. Check your attire and materials *before* the interview and then relax.

NAIL BITING

Once again, this could be a childhood habit, but it's interpreted as fear, nervousness or panic.

SWINGING OR TAPPING FEET

Your way of relaxing or coping in a situation can make you appear hurried and uninterested.

HANDSHAKES ARE IMPORTANT

As silly as it may sound, a handshake can secure—or lose—a job. I have actually had employers make their decision between two equally qualified candidates by the way they *shook hands.*

Some of the most frequently asked questions about the handshake are:

- **Should I extend my hand first?**
  Wait for the interviewer to

extend a hand first.

- **Should a man wait for a woman to extend a hand first?**
  Those days are gone forever.
  Use the guidelines above to
  determine who should initiate
  the handshake.

- **Should I move my hand up and down a few times when shaking?**
  No, it is not necessary to pump
  the arm, but a firm grip is
  important.

- **How hard should I squeeze?**
  Learn the answer to this one by
  trying—shake hands with a few
  people and ask them.

Handshakes are so important, some of them have actually been named. Here are the most basic:

- The **Dead Mackerel** suggests a weak personality.

- The **Bone Crusher** is too aggressive. The two-handed **Sandwich** is too personal for business.

- The **Grabber,** in which you grab the arm while shaking the hand, is too personal for a first meeting.

Now that you are frozen stiff, afraid to move for fear of insulting someone, relax. The bottom line on body language is this: *The person who exudes confidence, walks tall, looks you in the eye, has a firm handshake, and keeps the body movement minimal is most often trusted and accepted—and usually gets the offer.*

"Relax...I'm sure your name will come to you eventually."

SECRET #4

> *First* and *last*
> impressions *do*
> count.

FIRST AND FOREMOST

Your clothing and comments send a message. As the advertisement says, you'll never get another chance to make a first impression. People make immediate judgments about your economic level, education, trustworthiness, honesty and credibility all within that initial encounter. Amazingly enough, that critical first impression is usually made within *six seconds*.

Now that you know you have just six seconds, would you want to chance sending a mixed message?

Consider the woman who is interviewing for a position with a very professional and conservative law firm. She walks in with a beautiful suit that fits perfectly, matching pumps, a strand of pearls, small pearl earrings, her hair pulled back. But as she extends her hand for a handshake, the interviewer notices that each of her perfectly polished nails is extremely long and decorated with a design to match her suit. The interviewer can't help but wonder, "Is this a hard worker? How can she type on the computer? Is she too flashy for this office?"

Or take the gentleman interviewing for a position with an aggressive company. His suit is beautifully tailored, his tie spotless, his shoes shined, his hair clean and trimmed. When his potential employer walks over to introduce himself, however, the candidate looks away and never really makes eye contact during the entire interview. Mixed message? Absolutely. That one blunder could cost him the job, and he might never know why!

I'm sure you get the picture. *Concentrate on the total package.* Now let's think about *your* first impression.

Take some time right now to read each question and jot down your answer on the lines below.

1. How would you want someone to
    describe your appearance?

    _____

    _____

    _____

2. How would you describe a
    professional appearance?

    _____

    _____

    _____

3. How does a person portray
    self-confidence?

    _____

    _____

    _____

4. Name one person you feel has
    the "look" you would like to
    portray.

    _____

Why?

_____

_____

_____

These questions might give you some insight into how you feel about your image and how important it is to you. This may sound redundant, but remember that *first impressions do count* and are made within six seconds.

LASTING IMPRESSIONS

When the employer starts walking you out or is obviously ending the interview, you'll have your one and only shot at making your *last* impression.

Look the interviewer right in the eye and mention or repeat things you like about the company. These may be things the interviewer shared with you during the meeting, such as, "This is a growing company," "We believe in teamwork," or "We believe in quality, not just quantity."

Then ask for the job. *Do not leave an interview until you "close" on yourself and ask for the offer.* We'll talk more about closing later, because it's the most important part of the interview.

Your work doesn't end after you leave the building, however. Always send a handwritten thank-you note as a professional follow-up.

You or someone else should proofread carefully for spelling and grammatical errors. Top candidates have actually lost the job because they sent a thank-you note with a spelling error. Consider the two sample thank-you notes at the end of this chapter. Which candidate "closed" in the note?

Thomas Doe's note was the same old one everyone sends. Nothing stands out, so neither will this candidate.

Jane Doe, however, asked for the job. The old cliche, "If you don't ask, you don't get" is really true in a competitive market.

GLOWING RECOMMENDATIONS

References are always the *last* impression that clinches—or cools—the deal. When you provide references, make sure each person has been asked ahead of time and can be relied upon to give *glowing* references.

Often people fear a bad reference from a former employer because of personality conflict, a change in management or incompatibility, and omit the company or reference altogether. If you think your immediate supervisor might not give you the best reference, cover yourself by having another person at the company on your reference list.

So start out on the right foot by giving the best first impression possible, and let your references win the race for you by communicating your value to your potential employer.

THOMAS DOE
1234 S. 5th Street
Phoenix, AZ 87654
(602) 123-4567

December 17, 1992

Mr. Theodore Buckner
ARTIS LUGGAGE CO.
4598 W. Mockingbird Blvd.
Chattanooga TN 45667

Dear Mr. Buckner:

Thank you for your valuable time today. I enjoyed seeing how your company operates.

I hope to hear from you soon concerning the position.

Sincerely,

Thomas Doe

Thomas Doe

This thank-you note is the kind most people send

Jane Doe
1234 S. 5th St.
Phoenix AZ 87654
(602) 123-4567

December 19, 1992
Mr. Theodore Buckner
ARTIS LUGGAGE CO.
4598 W. Mockingbird Blvd.
Chattanooga TN 45667

Dear Mr. Buckner:

I just wanted to share with you my enthusiasm about the position and your company.

I was pleased to hear that you foster a team atmosphere and that I would be given a variety of responsibilities.

If given the offer, I am available to start immediately.

Sincerely,

Jane Doe
Jane Doe

This thank-you note asks for the job

SECRET #5

> **Always fill out
> company
> applications
> completely.**

You finally have a few face-to-face interviews lined up.

You arrive at the interview only to find out that you need to fill out an application. Should you just write "see resume" in every box? After all, they have your resume, so why fill out another form?

*BECAUSE IF YOU DON'T, YOU
COULD LOSE AN OPPORTUNITY.*

Some companies actually judge a candidate by how they fill out the company application!

They assess:

- Was it neat?

- Was it detailed?

- Was it thorough?

Even if it seems redundant, fill out the application each time with vigor and detail. Fill in every box with something, even if it's "N/A" for "not applicable." If a company has an application, it probably has a reason.

As you return the application to the receptionist, smile and be friendly. Remember who she works for—that's right, the company you are interviewing with—so don't treat her lightly. Some employers ask their receptionists what they thought of each candidate while they were waiting, and for good reason. Surprisingly, *most* people show two different personalities: one to the receptionist (who doesn't matter to them) and one to the employer.

So *treat receptionists with respect and warmth.* Their vote could be the final one.

SECRET #6

> **Interviewing is a
> numbers game, so
> know your numbers.**

Anyone making a career change needs to know the statistics of interviewing. (If we were gamblers, we'd call them odds and tell you that this book stacks them in your favor, but I prefer to look at it as keeping the chance-taking to a minimum.)

Understanding these "facts of interviewing" may release some of the pressure that goes along with the game, and who wouldn't like less stress in their life?

First of all, what is a "game"? According to a popular dictionary, a game is "a competitive activity governed by specific rules or the total number of points required to win the game."

That definition makes it clear that interviewing is indeed a game. The rules are already established before you start, even though most people don't know them.

Imagine playing any game and not knowing the rules! How could you possibly expect to win, or if you did, how would you even know?

If interviewing is a numbers game, then being aware of how many interviews, resumes, handshakes, buildings and companies you must encounter before you find the right job is an important rule in this game.

The following numbers, based on a large metropolitan area, have been studied for several years. They do change depending on the time of year, economy, etc., so what you see are averages:

You have to send out 32 resumes to get 1 response.

You have to send out 47 resumes to get 1 live interview.

You have to go to 21 interviews before you get an offer.

At our company, employers pay
us to find the perfect match.
We usually interview 85 people
a week

to send 20 to our client
companies.

Of the 20 candidates sent out,

approximately 8 will get a job offer.

These numbers could discourage you, but
my hope is that they will help you better understand rejections. Most "no thank yous"
aren't personal, you just have to do your
numbers.

Just remember that the greater the numbers in your networking, the better your
chances of having a "choice" when it's time
to make your career decision.

SECRET #7

There are only 20
basic questions
asked during any
interview.

Whether the job is white- or blue-collar, high-paying, moderate or modest, full- or part-time, conservative or creative, the same 20 questions are asked in nearly every interview.

Answer each in the space provided below, then read Secret #8 to see how you did.

The 20 most frequently asked questions are:

1. **Tell me about yourself.**

_____

_____

_____

2. **Where do you see yourself one year from now, or what are your career goals?**

_____

_____

_____

3. **What do you expect from a job?**

_____

_____

_____

4. **What is your best quality, or what is your greatest asset?**

_____

_____

_____

5. What is a quality you need to develop, or what is your worst quality?

   _____

   _____

   _____

6. What would you consider an ideal job for you?

   _____

   _____

   _____

7. Give two reasons why I should hire you.

   _____

   _____

   _____

8. What do you know about our company? What can you do for us?

   _____

   _____

   _____

9. **What kind of salary are you looking for?**

_____

_____

_____

10. **Would you consider less?**

_____

_____

_____

11. **What have you done that shows initiative?**

_____

_____

_____

12. **Who has influenced your life?**

_____

_____

_____

13. How do you define success?

_____

_____

_____

14. What major problems have you faced in your career, and how have you solved them?

_____

_____

_____

15. Which is more important to you: money or the type of job?

_____

_____

_____

16. Why have you held so many (or so few) jobs in the past six years?

_____

_____

_____

17. What did you like most about
    your last job? Least?

    _____

    _____

    _____

18. What did you like most and
    least about your last manager?

    _____

    _____

    _____

19. Why did you leave? (Sometimes
    they ask about each job, so be
    prepared.)

    _____

    _____

    _____

20. Why did you move (if you have
    relocated)?

    _____

    _____

    _____

SECRET #8

> **How you answer those 20 basic questions can give—or take away—your competitive edge.**

Now that you know the questions, let's discuss the answers. Once again, if you're prepared, you'll have an advantage over all the other candidates.

There are many correct ways to answer the most-frequently-asked questions. I *know*, however, that these answers work and continue to work over the years. I know not only because I've seen them work, but also because I've looked at them from the employer's viewpoint. And that's a valuable point: If you can put yourself on the employer's side of the desk, you will have a much better chance at getting the right position.

This chapter, then, is probably the most important chapter in the entire book. The answers we'll cover here will show you how you can answer each question honestly, yet maintain an advantage. (If you've ever been in a situation where you wanted to be totally honest, but it comes out all wrong, you'll know why this is valuable!)

So, in essence, here is the "teacher's manual" for the 20 basic interview questions:

1. Tell me about yourself.

Most people get tongue-tied on this one. For one thing, they don't know where to start. Should you go back to childhood? Should you discuss your personal life? Should you give dates? Here use the rule of thumb, "*Stick to business*," and emphasize anything pertinent to the particular job you're interviewing for.

Consider this appropriate answer (but make sure yours matches your situation!):

"I am dependable and a quick learner. I have two years' experience as an analyst. I'm looking for a company that will give me an opportunity to use my skills while helping the company achieve its goals."

2. **Where do you see yourself one year from now, or what are your career goals?**

Most people will respond with an honest answer such as, "I want to grow and advance with the company. I'm ambitious and eventually want to be in management, moving up the corporate ladder."

That sounds OK, until you put yourself in the employer's position. He or she is thinking, "This person wants to advance too quickly," or, "This person wants my job." Or perhaps, "This person is not willing to do the job for which we are interviewing for as long as we need them in that position."

Employ this rule of thumb: Be

honest, but be generic.

Consider:

*"After a year with the company,
I'll probably be looking for
additional responsibility because
I'm a person who enjoys a
challenge. I would like to be
paid accordingly for that
responsibility but, most
importantly, I'm looking for a
company I can be with for years
to come."*

3. What do you expect from a job?
Be honest, but remember that
growth and advancement are *ta-
boo.*

*"I expect to be given respect as
an employee and as a person. I
like to feel appreciated when a
job is well done."*

**4. What is your best quality, or
what is your greatest asset?**
Use a quality that would be
beneficial to the employer for this

job. For instance, if it's a management position, your best quality could be "motivating others," "delegating" or "being fair." If you're applying for a receptionist position, your answer could be "my telephone skills" or "a warm and patient personality."

5. **What is a quality you need to develop, or what is your worst quality?**

    This question calls for a positive negative:

    "I'm a perfectionist. I always want things done perfectly, although I realize I have to allow others to make mistakes."

    Or:

    "I'm always early for appointments instead of just being on time, and sometimes people aren't prepared."

6. **What would you consider an ideal job for you?**

    If possible, be general. The moment you get specific, you limit yourself.

Take, for example, a specific answer such as, "I would be working independently with numbers and learning a new computer system."

A safer answer would be: *"My ideal job would be a position where I feel I am contributing and productive, and where I'd be learning new things about my job and the company."*

7. Give two reasons why I should hire you.

Employers want to hear words such as "loyal," "dependable," "team player," "efficient," "workaholic," "dedicated," "organized," "effective." Be careful, however, to only use words that truly apply. Otherwise you start off on the wrong foot, trying to be something you are not.

You can become more specific when your qualities or technical abilities match the position:

*"I could increase company profit
and productivity in six months
with my production scheduling
experience and management
skills."*

8. **What do you know about our
   company? What can you do for us?**
   Do your homework. Quite
   often the local library or Better
   Business Bureau can provide
   valuable information about a
   company. But do make an effort,
   even if you have to do it in the
   waiting room by asking the receptionist questions such as, "How
   many employees does the company have?" "How long has the
   company been in business?" "Are
   there other companies with similar goals?" Employers are impressed when you care enough to
   check them out. They then know
   you are sincere about looking for
   a permanent home for yourself.
      Then you can respond to this
   question intelligently:
   *"I'm eager to learn more, but I
   do know the company was
   founded in 1946 by the
   Saunders family, that you now*

have three divisions in two
states, that you have more than
6,000 employees, and that you
pride yourselves on service.
Providing top-notch service is
certainly part of my philosophy,
and that's one of the reasons I
feel I will fit in well here."

9. What kind of salary are you looking for?

This is the most dreaded question of all and yet one of the most important. There are two good responses:

"I have been interviewing for
positions ranging between
$_____ and $_____.
However, finding the right
company is really most
important to me, because I plan
to be with that company a long
time."

Or:

"I'm currently at $_____, so
I'd like to at least make a
lateral move. Finding the right
company for my future, however,
is what is most important to me."

Both of these responses give a figure, but they also show some flexibility so you don't lose out on an opportunity because of miscommunication. Your goal is to get the offer. You can always accept or reject it, but without an offer, you don't have a decision.

10. Would you consider less?
Respond with a question.
"When are your salary reviews?"

Or:
"What figure did you have in mind?"

Or:
"A lot depends on your benefit package. Could you explain that to me?"

Notice how asking a question gets you out of the "hot seat" and back in control.

11. What have you done that shows initiative?
Choose something that will exhibit an ability you'd use in the position you are interviewing for,

such as:
"I read the computer tutorial and documentation at home and taught myself the new software package the company just purchased."

12. Who has influenced your life?
Be prepared with the name of your mentor or idol and the reason their influence has made a difference so you aren't caught off guard.

For example:
"Armand Hammer, the industrialist, has set an example for me. He not only made a fortune through brilliant business deals, he also influenced our world through diplomacy. I didn't always agree with his beliefs, but I do admire the way he worked to make the world a better place for all people."

13. How do you define success?
You may have your own answer for this one but if not, here are a couple that are sincere and to the point:

*"Success to me is doing exactly
what makes me happy."*

*"Success is feeling good about
myself."*

*"Success is setting personal
goals and attaining them."*

14. **What major problems have you
    faced in your career, and how
    have you solved them?**
    Once again, if you have had a
    major problem, try to be general.
    For instance, if you had
    trouble with your boss and finally
    quit, you might say:
    *"I worked with someone who had
    different principles and standards,
    and I learned that sometimes you
    have to walk away from a
    situation in order to grow
    personally. This was especially
    tough for me, because I'm usually
    persistent and very loyal."*

15. **Which is more important to
    you: the money or the type of job?**
    Straddle this one:

"Both, to a degree. If I'm not happy doing a particular job, then no amount of money would be sufficient. If, however, the money is right but I'm bored or just not feeling good about myself, then the money doesn't matter in the long run."

16. Why have you held so many (or so few) jobs in the past six years?
If this applies, be prepared. If you've moved or been transferred, your situation might be obvious, but the potential instability could cost you the job. So, whatever the reason for job hopping, reassure the employer that your No. 1 goal at this time is stability.
"I know it may look like I'm a job hopper, but there were a lot of circumstances beyond my control. The most important thing for me right now professionally is stability in both the company and my position."

17. What did you like most about

your last job?

This answer should fit the job for which you're applying. In other words, don't say, "a Fortune 500 atmosphere" if interviewing with a small company. Or, don't say, "interaction with co-workers" if the job requires you to work alone.

Try something such as:
"I enjoy paying attention to detail, the fast pace and the team atmosphere."

Least?

When answering the second part of this question, don't say, "managers," "my boss," "my co-workers" or anything else that puts down the company. The interviewer will immediately picture you saying something similar about this company the next time you're in the job market, so once again say something such as:
"It's more than 20 miles from my home."

Or:
"There wasn't enough work to keep me busy."

18. What did you like most about your last manager?

Again, be careful about being negative. For the first part of the question, consider:
"She was very challenging."

Least?

"I would have liked more feedback on the job I was doing."

19. Why did you leave?

Be truthful, but if it's too negative, such as you had a personality conflict, think of another way to say it.

"I felt I had stagnated professionally and, after discussing the situation with my boss, we both felt I would have more opportunity with another company. It was a mutual parting."

If you quit or were terminated and there was new management, you could also mention that there was a lot of turnover at that time.

20.Why did you move?

Instead of saying, divorce, death or some other negative that reveals your personal life (which is no one's business), it's best to say:

"I felt there are more opportunities here."

Or:

"I was seeking better weather."

Or:

"I wanted to be closer to family members."

Or:

"I was seeking a more dynamic community."

It helps to go through these questions with someone else or even alone just so you get used to hearing your voice. You'll learn to articulate the questions you seem to fumble over, and you'll become much more comfortable with them—and yourself.

When you're preparing for and finally in the interview, keep in mind that there are many different ways to ask the same question. If, however, you are prepared with the basic responses and realize that both parties want the same things (appreciation, stability, team orientation, dependability and loyalty), you will do very well on your interview.

Now compare your answers from the previous chapter!

"Other than your mother telling you it's time to get a job, can you tell me any other reason we should hire you?"

SECRET #9

> **Your purpose with *every* interview is to get an offer.**

When you read the secret above I imagine you thought:

- "What if I don't know if I even want an offer?"
- "I just started interviewing. Should I take the first offer?"
- "Don't I want to check out a lot of companies before I go for an offer?"

These are all valid concerns, but if there's anything important in this book, it's this:

IF YOU DON'T HAVE AN OFFER...
YOU DON'T HAVE A DECISION.

Just before candidates leave my office for an interview I ask them, "What is your purpose today in this interview?"

They usually answer, "I'm going to check out the company, see what they have to offer, and see if it's right for me."

Wrong.

Your purpose in an interview is to *get the offer.*

We'll explain the specifics of getting an offer in detail in the next chapter, but this is such an important point we want to keep this "secret" simple and clear.

Once the offer is on the table, you can decide if the company is right for you, if you fit in, and if it's where you want to be a year from now. But without the offer, you have no choice.

SECRET #10

**Second interviews
are as important as
the first.**

Most people prepare endlessly for the first meeting with a company. Then, other than choosing a different outfit, they often forget to prepare as much if not more so for the second. See this as your chance to close, to go for the offer, and begin a new chapter in your life.

On a second interview you will most likely meet a different person with different questions. Even if the second interview seems similar, believe me, it's different.

When I interview someone, I always have them back for a second meeting, because then the first impressions are behind us, and I can really make my decision about whether this person will "fit in."

In the previous chapter, we said your purpose is to get the offer.

YOU HAVE TO "CLOSE" ON THE SALE.
YOU HAVE TO "CLOSE" ON
YOURSELF.
YOU HAVE TO ASK FOR THE JOB.

Closing is a scary word to most people who are not in sales because it sounds so much like a "hard sales technique."

Before going on your next interview, you may want to practice closing, either with a friend or in front of a mirror. Adjust the wording to make it appropriate for your situation if you wish, but practice until you can ask for the offer confidently.

Here are four examples of asking for an offer that might make you more comfortable when making your pitch:

- "Mr. Employer, I've interviewed with several companies now and I know a good company when I see one. I hope you give me the opportunity to work with you in this company."

- "Ms. Employer, I enjoyed our time together. I especially liked the fact that your company is growing and you feel it's a family. I hope you will give me a chance to prove myself to you."

- "Mr. Employer, I am impressed with your company. I want this job, and I hope you will make me the offer."

- "Ms. Employer, I enjoy the atmosphere here, the job description sounds challenging, and I know I would be an asset to the company. I hope I'm the fortunate person who gets the offer."

Remember, if you don't ask you don't get, and this "*close*" could be the reason you get the job instead of one of the other candidates.

You have nothing to lose and everything to gain.

MOST-ASKED QUESTIONS ABOUT FOLLOW-UP INTERVIEWS

- **Should I wait to hear from the employer?**
  Follow up is up to you, not the prospective employer.

- **Should I send a thank-you note after each interview?**
  One thank-you note is sufficient as long as it's not redundant, and you make your point. Go for the close. Look at the example in Secret #4 and decide which person you would hire based on the follow-up note.

- **How long does it take most companies to make a decision?**
  This varies, but the average is two weeks from interview to offer to acceptance.

- **How long should I wait before following up on a resume I sent out?**
  My answer to this question has changed over the years. I used to feel you should call after four weeks, but I have discovered

*that it pays to be more
aggressive than that. Now I
recommend what I call*

THE 20/3 PLAN

1. *Look through the newspaper
    on Sunday. Circle 20 ads you
    are qualified for, and put a star
    by the three most interesting
    ones.*
2. *Send out resumes to the 20
    companies with a generic cover
    letter (see Secret #1).*

3. *Mark your calendar to check
    back 10 days later. Then send a
    follow-up letter to the three most
    interesting companies. The letter
    should ask if they received your
    resume and tell them that you
    are still interested and waiting
    to hear from them about the
    position.*
4. *If you haven't heard anything
    10 days after sending the
    follow-up letter, send the three
    companies a second follow-up.
    Tell them you are still available
    and are very interested in a
    face-to-face meeting with
    someone in the company.*

This program is surprisingly effective. Out of the hundreds of resumes a company receives, you will definitely be in the minority and stand a much better chance for a "live" interview.

I know this sounds like a lot of work and organization, but if you're looking for the job of your dreams to fall out of the sky, it just won't happen.

So get organized
DO YOUR NUMBERS
and
GET A JOB!

By the way, you can use this system weekly as the newspaper ads change...until you land a job.

TO ASK OR NOT TO ASK

At 99 percent of all interviews, the employer asks, "Do you have any questions?" What should you do?

We've talked about how interviewing is a game, but some people wonder if it's just one-sided. Many candidates want to ask questions, too, but such efforts can be dangerous because the wrong question could end the relationship.

For example, the interview went well. As it is ending, the employer asks, "Do you have any questions?"

You want to sound intelligent and, most importantly, interested, so you begin, "Now, about benefits..."

The employer starts pulling back from you, thinking that benefits are more important to you than the company or the job description. See what I mean by dangerous?

Here are five questions, however, that are

safe in any situation:

1. **"Is this a new position, or am I replacing someone?"**

2. **"Can you tell me what the person was like who formerly held this job?"**

3. **"Could you describe a typical work day?"**

4. **"If you could describe the personality that would best fit this job what would it be?"**

5. **"What do you think is the best thing and worst thing about this particular position?"**

Any of these questions conveys interest in the job without sending potentially problematic signals.

LAST-MINUTE TIPS BEFORE THE INTERVIEW

We discussed how important details are when preparing for an interview. Some of those details worth noting before embarking are:

- If you are just starting your career or haven't had much experience, tell the employer, "I am like a sponge. I am moldable and haven't already developed bad work habits."

- *Never* take friends or family on an interview with you.

- *Never* smoke, even if they ask you if you would like a cigarette.

- *Never* chew gum or suck on a breath mint during an interview.

You may think it's not noticeable, but it is.

- If the interviewer is not asking questions, it might be that he or she doesn't know what to ask. Remember to only offer information about yourself that pertains to the position you are interviewing for.

- Never leave the company without some sort of additional information. You can ask, "When will a decision be made?," "When can I expect to hear from you?," "Will I be informed of the decision either way?," or "How many other people are interviewing for this position?" At this point in your process you can even ask, "What do you think my chances are?"

Remember, you have nothing to lose and everything to gain by asking the right kind of questions and showing interest.

YOU ARE 'YOU-NIQUE'

By this time—especially if you read the chapter on numbers—you may be wondering, "Am I really special? Why would someone want me? What makes me unique?"

Even if you have a lot of self-confidence, it's still important to know how to sell the most important product of all: yourself.

Remember that rejection can be perceived however you choose.

During this interviewing game, try to see rejection as an elimination process. It doesn't matter whether that rejection comes from you or from the company, it only matters that you can now "let go" of that opportunity and move on to another one.

With that belief in mind, let's look at some of the things *you* need to consider before making a change in *your* career.

QUESTIONS TO ASK YOURSELF ABOUT YOUR POTENTIAL CAREER MOVE

If you are going to put a lot of time and effort into landing the perfect job, then you'd better make sure you are on the right track.

This is one time I can't tell you the "best" answer. You and only you know what works for you. So take 15 minutes to write down your responses so you understand yourself, and I promise it will help guide you to companies that will fulfill your goals.

- **Do I like small or large companies?**

  _____

  _____

  _____

- **Do I like to drive? How far (in minutes) is acceptable?**

  _____

  _____

  _____

- Do I want to work indoors or out-doors?

  _____

  _____

  _____

- Can I be in one location all day, or do I prefer to move about?

  _____

  _____

  _____

- Do I like to work alone, or do I need to be around other people?

  _____

  _____

  _____

- Should I be in a people-oriented environment?

  _____

  _____

  _____

- Do I thrive on stress, or should I look for a stress-free environment?

  _____

  _____

  _____

- What do I feel is the ideal position for me?

  _____

  _____

  _____

- What three things on the job are most important to me?

  _____

  _____

  _____

- Am I a self-starter, or do I need guidance?

  _____

  _____

  _____

- Do I have to be in charge, or do I mind working for someone else?

  _____

  _____

  _____

- Do I mind starting at entry level with a company?

  _____

  _____

  _____

- Am I a leader or a follower?

  _____

  _____

  _____

- Do I need to be dressed professionally everyday, or do I prefer to be casual?

  _____

  _____

  _____

- Is my work environment important
  to me? Does it need to be plush?
  Quiet? Have windows? Do I prefer
  my own office? etc.

  _____

  _____

  _____

- Out of all the positions I have
  held, which one gave me the most
  satisfaction?

  _____

  _____

  _____

- Do I enjoy working with an older
  group of people? All men? All
  women? People younger than me?
  etc.

  _____

  _____

  _____

Now add questions and answers that may
be pertinent to your own life and, when
you're done, you'll have a much clearer picture of your "perfect job."

WHERE TO FROM HERE?

Do you believe you are in total control of your life?

If you are like so many people, you'll probably reply, "You've gotta be kidding! Absolutely not."

Well, I'm here to tell you that you are. You can never control all the circumstances that are going to happen to you in this lifetime, but you *do* control your reactions to any given situation. That means *you actually do control your life and how you perceive it.*

Knowing this fact, I would like to close by sharing a special story with you.

> Once upon a time there was a wise old man who lived at the top of a mountain. This wise old man meditated and shared valuable insights about life with peo-

ple from a nearby village.

One day, three teenagers decided to trick the wise old man. One of the boys said, "This old man thinks he knows everything. Well, I'll show him. I'm going to hold a bird behind my back and ask the old man if the bird is alive or dead. If he says it's alive, I'll crush the bird. If he says it's dead, I'll let the bird fly."

With the plan set, the three boys climbed to the top of the mountain. There they saw the wise old man meditating in peaceful splendor. The boys walked over to the man, and the one boy asked, "Wise old man, what do I have in my hand?"

Because the wise old man knew everything, he continued looking straight ahead and said, "It's a bird, my son."

Now the boy winked at his two mates and said, "Wise old man, is the bird alive, or is it dead?"

The wise old man turned and looked the boy right in the eye and said, "The answer is in your hands, my son."

I tell you that story for many reasons, but mainly to convey that, like the boy with the bird, the answer to your destiny is in *your* hands. As you close the cover on this book, you have the choice to do several things:

- You can use the information for guidance
- You can share it with others, or
- You could actually destroy it, never to think of it again.

Just remember the Answer is in *your* hands.

I wish you success in whatever *you choose* to do.

Good luck!

Patricia

SUCCESS STORIES

"I was scared, confused and uncertain as to my future after being laid off due to company cutbacks. After reading Patricia's book I had a renewed sense of myself and what I needed to do to get the job of my dreams. By applying the valuable information in this book I convinced a national company to not only hire me but create a brand new position for me!"

—Joanne Collins
Little Falls, New York

"I recently moved to a new city and started looking for a job. I read the book the night before my interview and did everything just as the book said. I got the job and I love it! Thank you, Patricia Drain."

—Lori Hansen
Ames, Iowa

"As a recent graduate, the section on 'Sizzling Words for Resumes' helped me to add life to my resume and assisted me in making a more professional resume. In addition, Ms. Drain's sample interview questions were instrumental in building my confidence in approaching an interview."

        —Tiffany Finley
            University of Colorado
            1991 Graduate

"Thank you, Patricia Drain! Not only have you created the perfect ammunition for the challenging 'job jungle,' but you have offered an invaluable insight into the complexities of 'The Interview.' Armed with the knowledge and preparation for your book, I experienced positive results on my very first interview! I feel loaded with confidence, and that I have the 'secret' to the competitive edge over anyone who has not read 'The Secrets of Interviewing.'"

        —Jane Wilcox
            Manhattan, Kansas

"I highly recommend this book
to anyone who is interviewing.
It gave me the confidence and
control I needed. I knew what
to expect and what was expected
of me."
           —Sheila Higgason
            Chicago, Illinois

"Patricia Drain's book has been
instrumental to me in honing
my job search skills. While my
college education was thorough,
no aspect of the curriculum
addressed the skills I needed to
help me find my perfect job. The
book is so well written, clear and
concise and will continue to be of
great value to those interviewing.
It is interviewing made easy."
          —Rebecca F. Lodewyck
           Hemet, California

ABOUT THE AUTHOR

Patricia Noel Drain, Certified Personnel Consultant, founded Professional Perspectives, Inc., one of the largest and most respected employment services in Arizona. Her firm places and trains personnel with major local and national corporations.

Patricia has designed and presented professional attitude and image seminars, goal setting and productive time workshops and career development classes for both children and adults. She has spoken before numerous corporations and organizations, customizing topics to meet the needs of each group. Patricia also has a degree in education and has taught primary, secondary and adult students.

With a twenty-year background in Community Service and dedication to helping people through education, motivation and training, Patricia not only believes in the secrets within this book but is continually striving to assist individuals in finding the career of their dreams.

Patricia resides in Scottsdale, Arizona with her husband, Tom, daughter, Pamela and sons, Scott and Steven.